The Family Car Songbook

Running Press
Philadelphia, Pennsylvania

Canadian representatives: General Publishing Co. Ltd.
30 Lesmill Road, Don Mills, Ontario M3B 2T6

International representatives: Kaiman & Polon, Inc.
2175 Lemoine Avenue, Fort Lee, New Jersey 07024

9   8
Digit on right indicates the number of this printing.

This book may be ordered from the publisher. Please
include 75¢ postage. **But try your bookstore first.**
Running Press
125 South 22nd Street
Philadelphia, Pennsylvania 19103

Library of Congress Cataloging in Publication Data

The Family car songbook.
Without music.
Includes index.
Summary: Texts of songs of the "standard" variety, which lend themselves
to group singing.
1. Songs, English—United States—Texts.   2. Folksongs, English—United
States—Texts. 3. Children's songs—United States—Texts. 4. Music,
Popular (Songs, etc.)—United States—Texts.   [1. Songs]
M1627.F14   1983   83-3195
ISBN 0-89471-212-8 (paper)

Cover design by Jim Wilson
Cover illustration by Verlin Miller
Interior illustrations by Suzanne Clee
Researched and newly edited by Tam Mossman
Typography: Eras (by rci, Philadelphia, PA), and Benguiat
Printed by Port City Press, Baltimore, MD

CONTENTS (in alphabetical order)

OVER THE RIVER AND THROUGH THE WOODS

1. Over the river and through the woods
   To grandmother's house we go.
   The horse knows the way to carry the sleigh
   Through the white and drifted snow-oh!
   Over the river and through the woods
   Oh, how the wind doth blow!
   It stings the toes and bites the nose
   As over the ground we go.

2. Over the river and through the woods
   To have a real day of play.
   Oh, hear the bells ring,
   They ting-a-ling-ling,
   Because it's Thanksgiving Da-ay.

Over the river and through the woods
Trot fast, my dappled gray.
Spring over the ground just like a hound,
For this is Thanksgiving Day.

3. Over the river and through the woods
   And straight through the barnyard gate.
   We seem to be go-ing ever so slow.
   It's so very hard to wait!
   Over the river and through the woods
   Now grandmother's cap I spy.
   Hurrah for fun! Are the puddings done?
   Hurrah for the pumpkin pie!

RED RIVER VALLEY

1. From this valley they say you are going.
   We will miss your bright eyes and sweet smile,
   For they say you are taking the sunshine
   That brightens our pathway a while.

Chorus:
   Come and sit by my side if you love me.

Do not hasten to bid me adieu!
But remember the Red River Valley,
And the girl who has loved you so true.

2. For a long lonely time I've been waiting
   For those dear words you never did say,

But at last all my fine hopes have vanished,
For they say you are going away.

Chorus

3. Won't you think of the friends you are leaving?
Oh how lonely and sad they will be!
Won't you think of the heart you are breaking,
And the grief you are causing in me?

Chorus

4. From this valley they say you are going.
When you go, might your darling go too?
Would you leave her behind, unprotected,
When she cares for no other but you?

Chorus

5. I have promised you, darling, that never
Shall a word from my lips cause you pain.
And my life, it will be yours forever
If only you'll love me again.

Chorus

6. Must the past with its pleasures be blighted
By a love that must languish in vain?
Must the vows that were spoken be slighted?
Don't you think you can love me again?

Chorus

7. When you go off to live by the ocean,
May you never forget those sweet hours
That we spent in the Red River Valley,
Breathing love in the sun and the showers.

Chorus

8. Ne'er again could there rise such a longing
In the heart of a young maiden's breast.
And to that pure sweet love I'll be faithful
As I wait in my home in the West.

Chorus

9. Must you go now? Then take one last
blessing
From the Spirit that rules o'er the world:
May your pathways lie ever in sunshine,
Is the prayer of this Red River girl.

Chorus

10. They will bury me where you have
wandered,
On the hill where the daffodils grow,
When you're gone from the Red River Valley,
For I can't live without you, I know.

Chorus

FRÈRE JACQUES (Are You Sleeping?)

1. Frère Jacques, Frère Jacques,
   Dormez-vous?   Dormez-vous?
   Sonnez les matines, Sonnez les matines,
   Din, din, don!   Din, din, don!

2. [Traditional English translation:]

Are you sleeping?   Are you sleeping?
Brother John?   Brother John?
Morning bells are ringing,
Morning bells are ringing,
Ding, dong, ding!   Ding, dong, ding!

   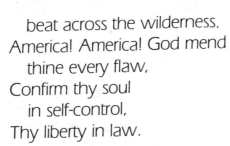

AMERICA THE BEAUTIFUL

1. Oh beautiful for spacious skies,
   For amber waves of grain,
   For purple mountain majesties
     above the fruited plain.
   America! America! God shed
     His grace on thee
   And crown thy good
     with brotherhood
   From sea to shining sea.

2. Oh beautiful for pilgrim feet
   Whose stern impassion'd stress
   A thoroughfare for freedom
   beat across the wilderness.
   America! America! God mend
     thine every flaw,
   Confirm thy soul
     in self-control,
   Thy liberty in law.

3. Oh beautiful for heroes proved
   In liberating strife,
   Who more than self
     their country loved
     and mercy more than life.
   America! America! May God
   thy gold refine
   Till all success be nobleness
   And every gain divine.

4. Oh beautiful for patriot dream
   That sees beyond the years.
   Thine alabaster cities gleam,
     undimmed by human tears.
   America! America! God shed
     His grace on thee
   And crown thy good
     with brotherhood
   From sea to shining sea.

THE OLD GRAY MARE

1. Oh, the old gray mare, she
Ain't what she used to be,
Ain't what she used to be,
Ain't what she used to be.
The old gray mare, she
Ain't what she used to be,
Many long years ago.

Chorus:
Many long years ago,
Many long years ago,
The old gray mare, she
Ain't what she used to be,
Many long years ago.

2. Oh, the old gray mare, she
Kicked on the wiffletree,
Kicked on the wiffletree,
Kicked on the wiffletree,
The old gray mare, she
Kicked on the wiffletree
Many long years ago.

THE MARINES' HYMN

1. From the Halls of Montezuma
To the shores of Tripoli,
We fight our country's battles
In the air, on land and sea.
First to fight for right and
   freedom
And to keep our honor clean,
We are proud to claim the title
Of United States Marine.

2. Our flag's unfurled to every
   breeze

From dawn to setting sun.
We have fought in every
   clime and place
Where we could take a gun.
In the snow of far-off
   northern lands
And in sunny tropic scenes,
You will find us always
   on the job—
The United States Marines.

3. Here's health to you and to
   our Corps
Which we are proud to
   serve.
In many a strife we've
   fought for life
And never lost our nerve.
If the Army and the Navy
Ever look at Heaven's scenes
They will find the streets
   are guarded
By United States Marines.

GREENSLEEVES

1. Alas, my love! You do me wrong
   To cast me off discourteously.
   For I have loved you so long,
   Delighting in your company.
   Greensleeves was all my joy.
   Greensleeves was my delight..
   Greensleeves was my heart of gold,
   Yea, who but my lady Greensleeves?

2. I have been ready at your hand,
   To grant whatever that you might crave.
   I have wagered both life and land,
   Your love and good-will for to have.
   If you intend thus to disdain,
   It doth the more enrapture me.
   And even so, I still remain
   Your lover in captivity.

3. My men were clothèd all in green,
   And they did ever attend on thee.
   All this was gallant to be seen,
   And yet, thou wouldst not love me.
   Thou couldst desire no earthly thing,
   But soon thou hadst it readily.

   Thy music still I play and sing,
   And yet thou wilt not love me.

4. Well, I shall petition God on high,
   That thou my constancy mayest see,
   And that yet once before I die,
   That thou wilt vouchsafe to love me.
   Ah, Greensleeves, farewell, adieu,
   And God, I trust, shall prosper thee.
   For I am still thy lover true.
   Come back once more and love me.

5. Ye watchful guardians of the fair,
   Who skim on wings of ambient air,
   Of my dear Delia take a care,
   And represent her lover
   With all the gaiety of youth,
   With honor, justice, love, and truth,
   Till I return, her passions soothe.
   For me in whispers move her.

6. Be careful no base sordid slave
   With soul sunk in a golden grave
   Who knows no virtue but to save
   With glaring gold bewitch her.

Tell her for me she was designed—
For me, who knows how to be kind,
And have more plenty in my mind
Than one who's ten times richer.

7. Let all the world turn upside-down
And fools run an eternal round
In quest of what can ne'er be found,
To please their own ambitions.
Let little minds great charms espy
In shadows which at distance lie,

Whose hoped-for pleasure,
    when come nigh,
Proves nothing in fruition.

8. But cast into a mold divine,
Fair Delia does with luster shine.
Her virtuous soul's an ample mine
That yields a constant treasure.
Let poets in sublimest verse
Employ their skills, her fame rehearse,
Let sons of music pass whole days
With well-tuned flutes to please her.

GO TELL AUNT RHODY

1. Go tell Aunt Rhody,
Go tell Aunt Rhody,
Go tell Aunt Rhody,
The old grey goose is dead—

2. The one that she's been
    fattening,
The one that she's been
    fattening,
The one that she's been
    fattening,

To make a feather bed.

3. She died last Thursday,
[Repeat twice.]
A sore pain in her head.

4. The old gander's mourning,
[Repeat twice.]
Because his wife is dead.

5. The goslings are weeping,
[Repeat twice.]
Because they've not been fed.

6. We'll have a funeral,
[Repeat twice.]
Is what the parson said.

7. She'll have a tombstone
[Repeat twice.]
To stand above her head.

8. And by the graveside,
[Repeat twice.]
We'll plant some roses red.

MY DARLING CLEMENTINE

1. In a cavern, in a canyon
   Excavating for a mine
   Dwelt a miner, Forty-Niner
   And his daughter,
     Clementine.

Chorus:
   Oh, my darling,
     oh my darling,
   Oh, my darling Clementine.
   You are lost and
     gone forever—
   Dreadful sorry, Clementine!

2. Light she was, and
     like a fairy,
   And her shoes
     were number nine.
   Herring boxes
     without topses,
   Sandals were for Clementine.

   Chorus

3. Drove she ducklings to
     the water
   Every morning just at nine.
   Struck her toe against
     a splinter,
   Fell into the foaming brine.

   Chorus

4. Ruby lips above the water
   Blowing bubbles
     soft and fine.
   Woe is me, I was
     no swimmer,
   So I lost my Clementine.

   Chorus

5. Then the miner, Forty-Niner
   He grew sad, began to pine,
   Thought he oughter
     "jine" his daughter.
   Now he's gone—like
     Clementine.

   Chorus

6. In a churchyard,
     near the canyon,
   Where the myrtle
     shoots entwine
   There grow rosies,
     'n' other posies
   Fertilized by Clementine.

   Chorus

7. In my dreams she
     still doth haunt me,
   Robed in garments
     soaked in brine.
   Though in life I
     used to hug her,
   Now she's dead,
     I'll draw the line.

   Chorus

THIS OLD MAN

1. This old man, he plays One.
   He plays nick-nack
     on my thumb.

Chorus:
   With a nick-nack,
   Paddy-whack,
   Give the dog a bone,
   This old man goes rolling
     home.

2. This old man, he plays Two.
   He plays nick-nack
     on my shoe.
       Chorus

3. This old man, he plays Three.
   He plays nick-nack
     on my knee.
       Chorus

4. This old man, he plays Four.
   He plays nick-nack
     on my door.
       Chorus

5. This old man, he plays Five.

He plays nick-nack
   on my hive.
     Chorus

6. This old man, he plays Six.
   He plays nick-nack
     on my sticks.
       Chorus

7. This old man, he plays
     Seven.
   Cross my heart and
     go to Heaven.
       Chorus

8. This old man, he plays Eight.
   He plays nick-nack
     on my gate.
       Chorus

9. This old man, he plays Nine.
   He plays nick-nack
     on my twine.
       Chorus

10. This old man, he plays Ten.

He plays nick-nack
   with his friends.
     Chorus

11. This old man, he plays
     'Leven.
   He plays nick-nack
     four and seven.
       Chorus

12. This old man, he plays
     Twelve.
   He plays nick-nack
     by himself.
       Chorus

13. This old man, he plays Teens.
   He plays nick-nack
     with string beans.
       Chorus

14. This old man, he plays
     Twenty.
   He plays nick-nack
     on my pennies.
       Chorus

I'VE BEEN WORKING ON THE RAILROAD

1. I've been working on the railroad
   All the livelong day.
   I've been working on the railroad,
   Just to pass the time away.
   Don't you hear the whistle blowing?
   Rise up so early in the morn!
   Don't you hear the foreman shouting?
   Dinah, blow your horn!

Chorus:

   Dinah, won't you blow?
      Dinah, won't you blow?
   Dinah, won't you blow your ho-o-orn?
   Dinah, won't you blow?
      Dinah, won't you blow?
   Dinah, won't you blow your horn?
   Someone's in the kitchen with Dinah,
   Someone's in the kitchen, I know-oh-oh-oh.
   Someone's in the kitchen with Dinah,
      Strumming on the old banjo.
   Fee, fie, fiddly-aye-oh,
   Fee, fie, fiddly-aye-oh-oh-oh-oh,
   Fee, fie, fiddly-aye-oh!

Strumming on the old banjo.

2. I've been working on the trestle,
   Driving spikes that grip.
   I've been working on the trestle,
   To be sure the ties won't slip.
   Can't you hear the engine coming?
   Run to the stanchion of the bridge!
   Can't you see the big black smokestack
   Coming down the ridge?

      Chorus

3. I've been living in the boxcars.
   I'm a hobo now.
   I've been living in the boxcars,
   Which the yard bulls won't allow.
   Brother, can you spare a quarter?
   Buy me something good to eat?
   Brother, can you spare a nickel,
   Till I'm on my feet?

      Chorus

4. I'll be owner of this railroad
   One of these here days.
   I'll be owner of this railroad,

And I swear, your pay I'll raise.
I'll invite you to my mansion,
Feed you on goose and terrapin.

I'll invite you to the racetrack
When my ship comes in.
Chorus

 # WHEN JOHNNY COMES MARCHING HOME AGAIN

1. When Johnny comes marching home again,
     Hurrah! Hurrah!
   We'll give him a hearty welcome then,
     Hurrah! Hurrah!
   The men will cheer, the boys will shout,
   The ladies they will all turn out.

Chorus:
   And we'll all feel gay when
   Johnny comes marching home.
   And we'll all feel gay when
   Johnny comes marching home.

2. The old churchbell will peal with joy
     Hurrah! Hurrah!
   To welcome home our darling boy.
     Hurrah! Hurrah!
   The village lads and lassies say

With roses they will strew the way.

     Chorus

3. Get ready for the Jubilee.
     Hurrah! Hurrah!
   We'll give the hero three times three.
     Hurrah! Hurrah!
   The laurel wreath is ready now
   To place upon his loyal brow.

     Chorus

4. Let love and friendship on that day
     Hurrah! Hurrah!
   Their choicest treasures then display.
     Hurrah! Hurrah!
   And let each one perform some part
   To fill with joy his warrior's heart.

     Chorus

WALTZING MATILDA

1. Once a jolly swagman
   Camped beside a billabong,
   Under the shade of a kulibah tree
   And he sang, as he sat and
   Waited till his billy boiled,
   "You'll come a-waltzing, Matilda, with me.

   Chorus:
   Waltzing Matilda,
   Waltzing Matilda,
   You'll come a-waltzing, Matilda, with me."

   And he sang, as he sat and
   Waited till his billy boiled,
   "You'll come a-waltzing, Matilda, with me."

2. Down came a jumbok
   To drink from a billabong
   Up jumped the swagman and shot it with glee,
   And he sang, as he stuffed the
   Jumbok in his tucker-bag,
   "You'll come a-waltzing, Matilda, with me.

   Chorus

   And he sang, as he stuffed the
   Jumbok in his tucker-bag,

   "You'll come a-waltzing, Matilda, with me."

3. Up rode the stockman
   Mounted on his thoroughbred.
   Up rode the troopers—one, two, three.
   "Where's the jolly jumbok you have in
      your tucker-bag?
   You'll come a-waltzing, Matilda, with me.

   Chorus

   Let us see the jumbok
   You have in your tucker-bag!
   You'll come a-waltzing, Matilda, with me."

4. Up jumped the swagman
   And leaped into the billabong.
   "You'll never catch me alive," said he.
   And his ghost may be heard
      as you pass by that billabong:
   "You'll come a-waltzing, Matilda, with me.

   Chorus
   And his ghost may be heard
      as you pass by that billabong:
   "You'll come a-waltzing, Matilda, with me."

[In American translation:]

5. Once a jolly drifter
Camped beside a waterhole
Under the shade of a broad spreading tree,
And he sang, as he waited
For his coffeepot to boil,
"You'll come a-swinging,
   my knapsack, with me.

Chorus:
   Knapsack a-swinging,
   Knapsack a-swinging,
   You'll come a-swinging,
      my knapsack, with me."

And he sang as he waited
For his coffeepot to boil,
"You'll come a-swinging,
   my knapsack, with me."

6. Down came a young lamb
To drink from the waterhole
Up jumped the hobo and shot it with glee.
And he sang, as he stuffed the
Young lamb in his duffel bag,
"You'll come a-swinging,
   my knapsack, with me.

Chorus

And he sang, as he stuffed the
Young lamb in his duffel bag,
"You'll come a-swinging,
   my knapsack, with me."

7. Up rode the ranchhand
Mounted on his fine black horse.
Up rode policemen—one, two, three.
"Where is that young lamb?
Is it in your duffel bag?
You and your knapsack,
   come swinging with me!

Chorus

Let's see the young lamb
You've got in your duffel bag.
You and your knapsack,
   come swinging with me!"

8. Up jumped the hobo
And plunged into the waterhole.
"You'll never take me alive," said he.
And his ghost you may hear
As you pass by that waterhole:
"You'll come a-swinging,

my knapsack, with me.

Chorus

And his ghost you may hear

As you pass by that waterhole:
"You'll come a-swinging,
  my knapsack, with me."

AMERICA! (My Country, 'Tis Of Thee)

1. My country! 'Tis of thee,
Sweet land of liberty,
Of thee I sing.
Land where my fathers died,
Land of the pilgrims' pride
From every mountainside
Let freedom ring.

2. My native country! Thee,
Land of the noble free,
Thy name I love.
I love thy rocks and rills,
Thy woods and templed hills.
My heart with rapture thrills,
Like that above.

3. Let music swell the breeze
And sing from all the trees

Sweet freedom's song.
Let mortal tongues awake,
Let all that breathe partake,
Let rocks their silence break,
The sound prolong.

4. Our father's God! To Thee,
Author of liberty,
To Thee we sing.
Long may our land be bright
With freedom's holy light.
Protect us by Thy might,
Great God our king.

5. God bless our native land.
Firm may she ever stand,
Through storm and night.
When the wild tempests rave,

Ruler of wind and wave,
Do Thou our country save,
By Thy great might.

6. For her our prayer shall rise
To God above the skies.
On Him we wait.
Thou, who are ever nigh,
Guarding with watchful eye,
To Thee aloud we cry,
"God save the state!"

7. Lord of all truth and right,
In Whom alone is might
On Thee we call.
Give us prosperity,
Give us true liberty.
May all th'oppressed go free.
God save us all!

I WISH I WERE IN DIXIE (Dixie Land)

1. I wish I were in the land of cotton.
   Old times there are not forgotten.
     Look away! Look away!
       Look away! Dixie Land.
   In Dixie Land where I was born in,
   Early on one frosty mornin'.
     Look away! Look away!
       Look away! Dixie Land.

Chorus:
   Then I wish I were in Dixie. Hooray! Hooray!
   In Dixie Land I'll take my stand,
   To live and die in Dixie.
   Away, away, away down south in Dixie,
   Away, away, away down south in Dixie.

2. Old Missus married Will the Weaver.
   William was a gay deceiver.
     Look away! Look away!
       Look away! Dixie Land.
   But when he put his arm around her,
   He smiled as fierce as a forty-pounder.
     Look away! Look away!
       Look away! Dixie Land.

Chorus

3. His face was sharp as a butcher's cleaver,
   But that did not seem to grieve her.
     Look away! Look away!
       Look away! Dixie Land.
   Old Missus acted the foolish part
   And died for a man that broke her heart.
     Look away! Look away!
       Look away! Dixie Land.

Chorus

4. Now here's a toast to the next old Missus,
   And all the girls that want to kiss us.
     Look away! Look away!
       Look away! Dixie Land.
   But if you want to drive 'way sorrow,
   Come and hear this song tomorrow.
     Look away! Look away!
       Look away! Dixie Land.

Chorus

5. There's buckwheat cakes and Injun batter,
   Makes you fat or a little fatter.

Look away! Look away!
Look away! Dixie Land.
Then hoe it down and scratch your gravel.
To Dixie Land I'm bound to travel.
Look away! Look away!
Look away! Dixie Land.
Chorus

6. Gonna cook a meal of grits and 'taters,

Feed what's left to the alligators.
Look away! Look away!
Look away! Dixie Land.
And when I die, see that they lay me
'Neath an oak that's cool and shady.
Look away! Look away!
Look away! Dixie Land.

Chorus

SHENANDOAH

1. Oh, Shenandoah, I love your daughter.
Away, you rolling river.
I'll take her cross yonder water.

Chorus:
Away, we're bound away.
'Cross the wide Missouri.

2. Oh, Shenandoah, she took my fancy.
Away, you rolling river.
Oh, Shenandoah, I love your Nancy.
Chorus

3. Oh, Shenandoah, I long to see you.

Away, you rolling river.
Oh, Shenandoah, I'm drawing near you.

Chorus

4. Oh, Shenandoah, I'm bound to leave you.
Away, you rolling river.
Oh, Shenandoah, I'll ne'er deceive you.

Chorus

5. Oh, Shenandoah, I'll ne'er forget you.
Away, you rolling river.
Oh, Shenandoah, I'll ever love you.

Chorus

FRANKIE AND JOHNNY

1. Frankie and Johnny were
   lovers.
   Oh, Lordy, how they could
   love!
   They swore to be true to
   each other,
   True as the stars above.
   He was her man,
   but he done her wrong.

2. Frankie, she was a good
   woman,
   And Johnny, he was
   her man.
   And every penny Frankie
   made
   Went right into Johnny's
   hand.
   He was her man,
   but he done her wrong.

3. Frankie and Johnny were
   sweethearts—

A fact 'most everybody
   knows.
   Frankie spent a hundred
   dollars,
   Just to buy her man
   some clothes.
   He was her man,
   but he done her wrong.

4. Frankie and Johnny went
   walking,
   Johnny in his brand-new suit.
   "Oh, my Lord," said Frankie,
   "Don't my Johnny
   look cute?"
   He was her man,
   but he done her wrong.

5. Frankie and Johnny,
   those lovers,
   They had a quarrel one day.
   Johnny up and told Frankie,
   "Bye-bye, I'm going away!"
   He was her man,
   but he done her wrong.

6. Johnny's old mother, she
   told him—
   A woman ever so wise—
   "Don't spend Frankie's
   money on
   That woman Nellie Bly.
   You're Frankie's man,
   and you're doin' her
   wrong."

7. Frankie rode down to
   Memphis,
   She went on the morning
   train.
   She left with a hundred
   dollars,
   Came back with a watch
   and chain,
   All for her man,
   who was doin' her wrong.

8. Frankie went down to
   the corner
   To buy her a glass of beer.

She said to the fat bartender,
"Has my lovin' Johnny
    been here?
    He is my man, and
    he wouldn't do wrong."

9. "I ain't gonna tell you
    no story,
    Ain't gonna tell you no lie.
    Johnny walked past 'bout
        an hour ago
    With a girl called Nellie Bly.
    If he's your man, then
        he's doin' you wrong."

10. Frankie went down to the
        pawnshop.
    She didn't go there for fun.
    She went and hocked all her
        jewelry,
    And bought a big forty-four
        gun
    For to shoot the man
        who was doin' her wrong.

11. Frankie walked up to the
        hotel,

Peeked in the window so
    high.
On a velvet couch sat
    Johnny
Loving up Nellie Bly.
    He was her man, and
    he was doin' her wrong.

12. Frankie went back to the
        front door,
    And leaned on that
        desk clerk's bell.
    "Out of my way, you
        floozies and fools,
    Or I'll blow you all to Hell.
    I want my man,
        who is doin' me wrong."

13. Frankie threw back
        her kimono,
    She took out the forty-four,
    Aimed at the ceiling
        and shot a hole
    Clean through that
        hardwood floor.

He was her man,
    but he done her wrong.

14. Johnny, he hears Frankie
        talking.
    Into the lobby he scoots.
    Frankie, she lifts up her pistol.
    "Frankie," says Johnny,
        "Don't shoot!
    'Cause I'm your man,
        though I done you
        wrong."

15. But Frankie, she pulled on
        the trigger.
    Frankie, she pulled it again.
    Rooty-toot-toot, three
        times she shoot
    While aiming at her man.
    He was her man,
        but she shot him down.

16. First time she shot him,
        he staggered.

Next time she shot him
   he fell.
Third time that she shot
   him, Lord,
There was a new man's
   face in Hell.
She killed that man,
   who had done her wrong.

17. "Oh, roll me over, Doctor.
Oh, turn me over slow.
Roll me over on my
   right side,
Where the bullet don't
   hurt me so.
I was her man,
   but I done her wrong."

18. Right away, Frankie
   was sorry.
It wrung her poor heart sore
To see her loving Johnny
Stretched out on that hotel
   floor,

'Cause he was her man,
   though he done her
   wrong.

19. She went to the undertaker's
And ordered up a coffin
   so wide,
All lined with pearl-grey satin—
The best that money
   could buy
To bury that man
   who had done her wrong.

20. Bring out your long black
   hearses.
Bring out your funeral clothes.
Johnny's laid out in
   the parlor.
To his wake poor Frankie
   goes.
He was her man,
   but he done her wrong.

21. Frankie, she stood by
   the coffin.
Frankie gazed down on
   his face.

Said, "Oh, Lord, have mercy
   on me—
I wish I could take his place.
He was my man,
   and I done him wrong."

22. Frankie saw Johnny's
   mother,
Went down on her knees,
Told her, "Mrs. Halcomb,
Won't you forgive me, please?
I killed your son,
   'cause he done me
   wrong."

23. "Forgive you, Frankie darlin'?
Forgive you I never can.
How can I forgive you, dear,
For shooting your only man?
He was your man,
   though he done you
   wrong."

24. Here come your rubber-tire
   hearses,
Here comes your horse-
   drawn hack.

Seven men went to the
   burying ground,
And only six came back.
   They planted the man
   who had done her wrong.

25. The sheriff came 'round
   in the morning.
"Frankie, it's all for the best.
That gambler Johnny
   Halcomb
Was just a doggone pest.
   He was your man,
   but he done you wrong."

26. Said Frankie, "Bring your
   policemen.
Bring 'em around today,
To lock me in a dungeon cell
And throw the key away.
   I shot my man,
   and I done him wrong.

27. "Yeah, lock me down in
   that dungeon.
Shut me up in that cell.
Put me where the north

wind blows
From the southwest corner
   of Hell.
   He was my man,
   and I done him wrong."

28. Frankie, she said to
   the warden,
"What are they going
   to do?"
"Frankie," the warden, he
   answered,
"It's the 'lectric chair for you.
   You killed your man,
   and you done great
   wrong."

29. Judge, he instructed the jury:
"It's plain as plain can be
That this woman shot her
   lover.
It's murder in the second
   degree!
   He was her man,
   and she shot him down."

30. But the jury didn't find

her guilty
Of murder in the second or
   third.
"This woman simply
   dropped her man,
Like a hunter drops a bird.
   He was her man,
   but he done her wrong."

31. Judge, he looked down on
   Frankie,
Under the electric fan.
Said the judge, "You're a free
   woman now.
Go shoot you a brand-new
   man.
   The deceased was yours,
   but he's dead and gone."

32. This story has no moral.
This story has no end.
This song only goes to show
That there's just no good
   in men.
   They'll do you wrong,
   as sure as you're born.

GIT ALONG, LITTLE DOGIES

1. As I was a-walking
   one morning for pleasure,
   I spied a cowpuncher
   come riding along.
   His hat was pushed back,
   And his spurs were a-jangling,
   And as he approached,
   he was singing this song:

Chorus:
   Yip-pee-yay, Hi yo!
   Git along, little dogies.
   It's your misfortune
   and none of my own.
   Yip-pee-yay, Hi yo!
   Git along, little dogies,

For you know Wyoming'll
   be your home.

2. It's early in spring when
   we round up the dogies,
   We rope 'em and brand 'em
   and bob off their tails,
   We water our ponies,
   load up the chuck-wagon,
   And then drive the dogies
   out onto the trail.

   Chorus

3. Some boys, they go out on
   the trail just for pleasure,
   But that's where they get it

most terribly wrong—
You'd never imagine
   the trouble they give us!
It takes all we've got
   to keep moving along.

   Chorus

4. It's yelling and whooping
   and driving the dogies,
   And oh, how we wish
   they would kindly move on.
   It's whooping and punching,
   and "Git on, little dogies,
   For you know Wyoming
   must be your new home."

   Chorus

TWINKLE, TWINKLE, LITTLE STAR

1. Twinkle, twinkle, little star.
   How I wonder what you are!

Up above the world so high,
Like a diamond in the sky.

Chorus:
   Twinkle, twinkle, little star.
   How I wonder what you are!

2. When the blazing sun
     goes down,
   Darkness falls all over town.
   Then you show your tiny light,
   Twinkling, twinkling,
     through the night.
   Chorus

3. Weary travellers in the dark
   Thank you for your little
     spark.
   Who could see which path
     to go,
   If you did not twinkle so?
   Chorus

4. In the dark sky you remain,
   Peeking through my
     windowpane.
   And you never close
     your eye
   Till the sun is drawing nigh.
   Chorus

 # THE YELLOW ROSE OF TEXAS

1. There's a Yellow Rose in Texas
   That I am going to see
   No other fellow knows her
   No, not a one but me.
   She cried so when I left her
   It like to broke my heart.
   And if I ever find her
   We never more will part.

Chorus:
   She's the sweetest rose in Texas
   That this man ever knew.
   Her eyes are bright as diamonds:
   They sparkle like the dew.

You may talk about your dearest May
And sing of Rosa Lee,
But the Yellow Rose of Texas
Beats the belles of Tennessee.

2. Where the Rio Grande is flowing
   And starry skies are bright,
   She walks along the river
   In the quiet summer night.
   She asks if I remember
   When we parted long ago,
   I promised to come back again,
   And not to leave her so.

Chorus

3. Oh, now I'm going to find her
   For my heart is full of woe.
   We'll sing the songs together
   We sung so long ago.

We'll play the banjo gaily,
We'll sing the songs of yore,
And the Yellow Rose of Texas
Will be mine forevermore.

Chorus

 # GOOBER PEAS

1. Sitting by the roadside
   On a summer's day,
   Chatting with my messmates
   Passing time away,
   Lying in the shadows,
      underneath the trees
   Goodness, how delicious
   Eating goober peas!

Chorus:
   Peas, peas, peas, peas!
   Eating goober peas!
   Goodness, how delicious,
   Eating goober peas!

2. When a horseman rides by,
   The soldiers have a rule

To cry out at their loudest,
"Mister, here's your mule!"
But another pleasure
   enchantinger than these
Is wearing out your grinders
Eating goober peas!

Chorus

3. Just before the battle
   The General hears a row.
   He says, "The Yanks
      are coming,
   I hear their rifles now!"
   He turns around in wonder,
      and what d'you think
      he sees?

The Georgia Militia
Eating goober peas!

Chorus

4. I think this song has lasted
   Almost long enough.
   The subject's interesting,
   But rhyming's mighty rough.
   I wish this war was over
      when, free from rags
      and fleas,
   We'll kiss our wives and
      sweethearts
   And gobble goober peas.

Chorus

THE ERIE CANAL

1. I've got a mule, her name is Sal.
   Fifteen miles on the Erie Canal.
   She's a good old worker and a good old pal.
   Fifteen miles on the Erie Canal.
   We've hauled some barges in our day,
   Filled with lumber, coal, and hay
   And we know every inch of the way
   From Albany to Buffalo.

Chorus:
   Low bridge, everybody down!
   Low bridge, for we're going through a town.
   And you'll always know your neighbor,
   And you'll always know your pal,
   If you've ever navigated on the Erie Canal.

2. We better get along on our way, old gal.
   Fifteen miles on the Erie Canal.
   'Cause you bet your life I'd never part with Sal.
   Fifteen miles on the Erie Canal.
   Get up there, mule, here comes a lock.
   We'll make Rome 'bout six o'clock.
   One more trip and back we'll go,
   Right back home to Buffalo.

Chorus

3. Now where would I be if I lost my pal?
   Fifteen miles on the Erie Canal.
   I'd like to see a mule half as good as Sal.
   Fifteen miles on the Erie Canal.
   A fool barge-cap'n once got her sore.
   Now he's got a broken jaw,
   'Cause she let fly with her iron shoe,
   And knocked him clear to Timbuctoo.

Chorus

4. You can hear them sing all about my gal.
   Fifteen miles on the Erie Canal.
   It's a right fine ditty 'bout my mule Sal.
   Fifteen miles on the Erie Canal.
   Every band will be playin' it soon—
   Darn fool words and a darn fool tune,
   But you'd better learn it before you go
   On board the barge at Buffalo.

Chorus

FUNICULI, FUNICULA

1. Some think the world is
      made for fun and frolic
   And so do I!
   And so do I!
   Some think
   It well to be all melancholic,
   To pine and sigh,
   To pine and sigh.
   But I, I love to spend
      my time in singing
   Some joyous song,
   Some joyous song.
   To set the air with music
      bravely ringing
   Is far from wrong,
   Is far from wrong!

   Chorus:
      Listen! Listen!
      Echoes sound afar!
      Listen! Listen!
   Echoes sound afar!
   Funiculi, funicula,
   Funiculi, funicula!
   Echoes sound afar!
   Funiculi, funicula!

2. Some think it wrong to set
      the feet a-dancing.
   But not so I!
   But not so I!
   Some think that eyes should
      keep from coyly glancing
   Upon the sly,
   Upon the sly.
   But oh, to me the mazy
      dance is charming,
   Divinely sweet,
   Divinely sweet!
   For surely there is nought
      that is alarming
   In nimble feet,
   In nimble feet!

   Chorus

3. Ah, me! 'Tis strange that
      some should take to
      sighing,
   And like it well,
   And like it well!
   For me, I have not thought
      it worth the trying,
   So cannot tell,
   So cannot tell!
   With laugh and dance and
      song the day soon passes,
   Full soon is gone,
   Full soon is gone!
   For mirth was made for
      joyous lads and lasses
   To call their own,
   To call their own!

   Chorus

 # THE STREETS OF LAREDO

1. As I walked out in
       the streets of Laredo,
   As I walked out
       in Laredo one day,
   I spied a poor cowboy
       wrapped in white linen,
   Wrapped up in white linen
       and cold as the clay.

2. "I see by your outfit
       that you are a cowboy."
   These words he did say
       as I boldly stepped by.
   "Come sit down beside me
       and hear my sad story—
   I was shot in the chest
       and I know I must die.

3. "Let sixteen gamblers come
       serve as my mourners.
   Let sixteen cowboys

   come sing me a song.
   Take me to the graveyard
       and lay the sod o'er me,
   For I'm a poor cowboy and
       I know I've done wrong.

4. "It was once in the saddle
       I used to go dashing.
   It was once in the saddle
       I'd ride all the day.
   'Twas first to drinking
       and then to card playing,
   Got shot in the chest,
       and I'm dying today.

5. "Get six jolly cowboys
       to carry my coffin.
   Get six pretty maids
       to carry my pall.
   Put bunches of roses
       all over my coffin,

   White roses to soften
       the clods as they fall.

6. "Oh, beat the drum slowly
       and play the fife lowly
   And play a sad dirge
       as you tote me along.
   Take me to the valley
       and lay the earth o'er me,
   For I'm a young cowpoke and
       I know I've done wrong."

7. We beat the drum slowly
       and played the fife lowly,
   And bitterly wept as
       we bore him along.
   For we all loved our comrade,
       so brave and so handsome,
   We all loved our cowboy
       although he'd done wrong.

SWEET BETSY FROM PIKE

1. Have you heard the tale
     of Sweet Betsy from Pike,
   Who crossed the high
     Rockies with her lover Ike,
   With two yoke of cattle,
     and one yaller dog,
   A tall Shanghai rooster,
     and one spotted hog?

Chorus:
   Saying, "Love you,
     Pike County,
   Farewell just the same.
   We'll be back again
   When we've panned
     out our claim."

2. One evening quite early,
     they camped by the
     Platte.
   'Twas close by the road
     on a green shady flat
   Where Betsy, quite tired,
     lay down to repose

While loving Ike gazed
  on his Pike County rose,

Alternate chorus:
   Sighing, "Goodbye,
     Pike County,
   Farewell for a while.
   We'll see you again
   When we've panned out
     our pile."

3. Came some Injuns on horse-
     back, a wild yelling horde.
   And they terrified Betsy,
     who prayed to the Lord.
   Beneath their big wagon
     the couple did crawl
   And drove off the Injuns
     with musket and ball.

   Chorus

4. They trudged the deep valleys
     and crossed the tall peaks,
   And lived off of berries
     and water for weeks,

And nearly got drowned
  in a fast mountain stream,
For to reach California
  was their only dream.

   Alternate chorus

5. The rooster ran off and
     the cattle all died.
   Their last strip of bacon
     that morning they fried.
   Poor Ike was discouraged,
     and Betsy was mad.
   The dog wagged his tail and
     looked wonderfully sad.

   Chorus

6. They soon hit the desert,
     where Betsy gave out,
   And in the hot sands she
     lay, rolling about,
   While Ike cried hot tears,
     looking on in surprise,
   And said, "Betsy, get up—
     you'll get sand in

your eyes."

Alternate chorus

7. Sweet Betsy rose up
    in considerable pain,
And said she'd return
    to Pike County again,
But Ike shook his head,
    and they fondly
    embraced,
And onward she traveled,
    his arm 'round her waist,

Chorus

8. One morning they climbed up
    a very high hill,
And with wonder looked
    down into old Placerville.
Ike shouted and said,
    as his eyes down he cast,
"Sweet Betsy, my darling,
    we've made it at last."

Alternate chorus

9. Long Ike and sweet Betsy
    attended a dance,

Where Ike wore a pair
    of his Pike County pants.
Sweet Betsy was all
    dressed up in ribbons
    and rings.
Said Ike, "You're an angel,
    but where are your
    wings?"

Chorus

10. A miner asked, "Betsy,
    will you dance with me?"
"I will," she replied,
    "if you don't make too
    free,
And don't dance me too
    hard. Do you want to
    know why?
Doggone you, I'm brim-full
    of strong alkali."

Alternate chorus

11. Long Ike and sweet Betsy
    got married in May.
And dwelled in a shack
    in the hills, so they say.

After six months in 'Frisco,
    Long Ike met a girl—
A sweet-looking dancer
    who gave him a whirl.

Chorus

12. Ike spoke of poor Betsy
    as "just an old horse."
What was Betsy to do?
    She gave Ike a divorce.
Once more a free woman,
    she said with a shout,
"Goodbye, you big lummox,
    it's time you cleared out."

Alternate chorus

13. Well, Betsy went back
    to Pike County that May,
And Ike lost his dancer
    and soon passed away.
If this story's too sad,
    you can cry if you like
For that mighty fine woman,
    sweet Betsy of Pike.

Chorus

YANKEE DOODLE

1. Father and I went down to camp
   Along with Captain Goodwin
   And there we saw the men and boys
   As thick as hasty pudding.

Chorus:
   Yankee Doodle, keep it up!
   Yankee Doodle Dandy,
   Mind the music and the step,
   And with the girls be handy.

2. And there we saw a thousand men,
   As rich as Squire David
   And what they wasted every day,
   I wish it could be savèd.

   Chorus

3. And there was Captain Washington
   Upon a strapping stallion
   A-giving orders to his men—
   I guess there was a million.

   Chorus

4. And then the feathers on his hat,
   They looked so very fine, ah!
   I wanted one of them to get,

To give to my Jemimah.

   Chorus

5. And there I saw a swamping gun,
   Large as a log of maple,
   Upon a mighty little cart,
   A load for father's cattle.

   Chorus

6. And every time they fired it off,
   It took a horn of powder.
   It made a noise like father's gun,
   Except a whole lot louder.

   Chorus

7. And there I saw a little drum,
   Its heads all made of leather.
   They knocked upon't with little sticks
   To call the troops together.

   Chorus

8. And Captain Davis had a gun,
   He clapped his hand upon it,
   And stuck a crooked stabbing iron
   Upon the little end on't.

Chorus

9. And Uncle Sam came there to charge
Some pancakes and some onions
And 'lasses cakes to carry home
To give his wife and young ones.

Chorus

10. And there they'd fife away for fun
And play on cornstalk fiddles
And some wore ribbons red as blood
Bound tight around their middles.

Chorus

11. The troopers, too, would gallop up
And shoot right in our faces.
It scared me almost half to death
To see them run such races.

Chorus

12. It scared me so that I ran off,
Nor stopped, as I remember,
Nor turned about till I got home,
Locked up in mother's chamber.

Chorus

ON TOP OF OLD SMOKY

Chorus:
   On top of old Smoky,
   All covered with snow,
   I lost my true lover
   From a-courtin' too slow.

1. On top of old Smoky
   I went for to weep,

For a false-hearted lover
Is worse than a thief.

[Chorus optional]

2. For a thief, he will rob you
   Of all that you have,
   But a false-hearted lover

Will send you to your grave.

[Chorus optional]

3. He'll hug you and kiss you
   And tell you more lies
   Than the ties of the railroad
   Or the stars in the skies.

HUSH, LITTLE BABY

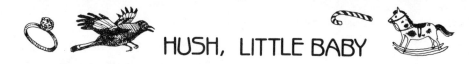

1. Hush, little baby, don't say a word,
   Daddy's gonna buy you a mocking bird.
   If that mocking bird don't sing,
   Daddy's gonna buy you a diamond ring.

2. If that diamond ring is brass,
   Daddy's gonna buy you a looking glass.
   If that looking glass gets broke,
   Daddy's gonna buy you a nanny goat.

3. If that goat don't give no milk,
   Daddy's gonna buy you a robe of silk.
   If that robe of silk gets worn,
   Daddy's gonna buy you a big French horn.

4. If that big French horn won't play,
   Daddy's gonna buy you a candy cane.
   If that cane should lose its stripes,
   Daddy's gonna buy you a set of pipes.

5. If that set of pipes ain't clean,
   Daddy's gonna buy you a jumping bean.
   If that jumping bean won't roll,
   Daddy's gonna buy you a lump of coal.

6. If that lump of coal won't burn,
   Daddy's gonna buy you a butter churn.
   If that butter turns out sour,
   Daddy's gonna buy you an orchid flower.

7. If that flower don't smell sweet,
   Daddy's gonna buy you some salted meat.
   If that salted meat won't fry,
   Daddy's gonna buy you an apple pie.

8. When that apple pie's all done,
   Daddy's gonna buy you another one.
   When that pie's all eaten up,
   Daddy's gonna buy you a greyhound pup.

9. If that dog won't run the course,
   Daddy's gonna buy you a rocking horse.
   If that rocking horse won't rock,
   Daddy's gonna buy you a cuckoo clock.

10. And if that cuckoo clock runs down,
    You're still the prettiest little girl in town.

HOME ON THE RANGE

1. Oh, give me a home where the buffalo roam,
   Where the deer and the antelope play,
   Where seldom is heard a discouraging word,
   And the sky is not clouded all day.

Chorus:

   Home, home on the range!
   Where the deer and the antelope play,
   Where seldom is heard
   A discouraging word,
   And the sky is not clouded all day.

2. Oh, give me a gale
      on some soft Southern vale,
   Where the stream of life joyfully flows,
   On the banks of the river,
      where seldom if ever,
   Any poisonous herbiage grows.

      Chorus

3. Oh, give me a land where the bright
      diamond sands
   Lie awash in the glittering stream,
   Where days glide along in leisure and song,

And afternoons pass as a dream.

   Chorus

4. I love the bright flowers in this frontier of ours,
   And I thrill to the eagle's shrill scream.
   Blood red are the rocks,
      brown the antelope flocks
   That browse on the prairie so green.

      Chorus

5. The breezes are pure, and the sky is azure,
   And the zephyrs so balmy and slow,
   That I would not exchange
      my home on the range
   For a townhouse in San Francisco.

      Chorus

6. How often at night,
      when the heavens are bright
   With the light of the unclouded stars,
   Have I stood here amazed
      and asked, as I gazed,
   If their glory exceeds that of ours.

      Chorus

THE JOHN B. SAILS (The Sloop John B.)

1. Oh, we came on the sloop
   John B.,
   My grandfather and me.
   'Round Nassau Town
   we did roam.
   Drinking all night,
   we got into a fight.
   I feel so broke up,
   I want to go home.

Chorus:
   So hoist up the John B. sails.
   See how the mainsail sets.

Send for the Captain ashore.
Let me go home!
Let me go home,
Let me go home.
I feel so broke up,
   I want to go home.

2. The first mate, he got drunk,
   Broke up somebody's trunk.
   Constable came aboard
   and took him away.
   Sergeant John Stone,
   please leave me alone.

I feel so broke up,
   I want to go home.

Chorus

3. The poor cook, he got fits,
   Threw 'way all of the grits,
   Then he took and ate up
   all of my corn.
   Let me go home,
   I want to go home.
   This is the worst trip
   since I've been born.

 LITTLE BROWN JUG

1. My wife and I lived all alone,
   In a little log hut
   we called our own.
   She loved gin,
   and I loved rum.
   I tell you what,

   we'd lots of fun!
Chorus:
   Ha, ha, ha, you and me,
   Little brown jug,
   don't I love thee.
   Ha, ha, ha, you and me,

Little brown jug,
   don't I love thee.
2. 'Tis you who makes
   my friends my foes
   'Tis you who makes me
   wear old clothes,

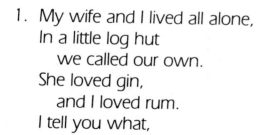

Here you are,
  so near my nose,
So tip her up,
  and down she goes.
  Chorus

3. When I go toiling
    to my farm,
  I take little brown jug
    under my arm.
  I place it under a shady tree.
  Little brown jug,
    'tis you and me.
  Chorus

4. If all the folks in Adam's race
  Were gathered together
    in one place,
  Then I'd prepare
    to shed a tear
  Before I'd part from you,
    my dear.
  Chorus

5. If I'd a cow that
    gave such milk,
  I'd clothe her in
    the finest silk.
  I'd feed her on

  the choicest hay,
  And milk her forty
    times a day.
  Chorus

6. The rose is red;
    my nose is, too.
  The violet's blue,
    and so are you.
  And yet I guess before I stop,
  We'd better take
    another drop.
  Chorus

DOWN BY THE RIVERSIDE

1. Going to lay down my sword and shield,
  Down by the riverside,
  Down by the riverside,
  Down by the riverside.
  Going to lay down my sword and shield,
  Down by the riverside,
  Down by the riverside.

Chorus:
  I ain't going to study war no more,
  I ain't going to study war no more,
  I ain't going to study war no more!
  I ain't going to study war no more,
  I ain't going to study war no more,
  Down by the riverside.

2. Going to lay down my heavy load,
   Down by the riverside,
   [Repeat as above, followed by chorus.]

3. Going to ride on a milk-white horse,
   Down by the riverside,
   [Repeat as above, followed by chorus.]

4. Going to try on a snow-white robe,
   Down by the riverside,
   [Repeat as above, followed by chorus.]

5. Going to put on my starry crown,
   Down by the riverside,
   [Repeat as above, followed by chorus.]

6. Getting ready to meet my Lord,
   Down by the riverside,
   [Repeat as above, followed by chorus.]

THE HAPPY WANDERER

1. I am a happy wanderer
   Along the mountain track,
   And as I go, I love to sing,
   My knapsack on my back.

Chorus:
   Val-de-ri, Val-de-rah,
   Val-de-ri, Val-de-rah—
      ha, ha, ha, ha, ha,
   Val-de-ri, Val-de-rah,
   My knapsack on my back.

2. I love to wander by the stream

That dances in the sun.
So joyously it calls to me,
"Come join my happy song."

   Chorus

Come join my happy song.

3. I wave my hat to all I meet,
   And they wave back to me.
   And blackbirds call so
      loud and sweet
   From every greenwood tree.

   Chorus

From every greenwood tree.

4. Oh, may I go a-wandering
   Until the day I die.
   Oh, may I always laugh
      and sing
   Beneath God's clear blue sky.

   Chorus

Beneath God's clear blue sky.

THE BIG ROCK CANDY MOUNTAIN

Chorus:
Oh, the buzzing of the bees
In the cigarette trees
And the soda water fountain,
By the lemonade springs where the
bluebird sings
In the big rock candy mountain!

1. On a warm spring day in the month of May,
A burly bum came hiking
Down a shady lane near the sugar cane.
He was looking for his liking.
As he strolled along, he sang a song
Of a land of milk and honey
Where a bum can stay for many a day,
And he won't need any money.

Chorus

2. In the big rock candy mountain,
All the cops have wooden legs.
The bulldogs all have rubber teeth
And the hens lay soft-boiled eggs.
The farmers' trees are full of fruit,

And the barns are full of hay.
Oh, I want to go where there ain't no snow,
Where the sleet don't fall
and the rain don't blow,
In the big rock candy mountain!

Chorus

3. In the big rock candy mountain,
You need never change your socks.
And fizzy streams of fine champagne
Come trickling down the rocks.
The boxcars all are empty,
And the railroad bulls are blind.
There's a lake of stew and ginger ale too.
You can paddle all 'round in a big canoe,
In the big rock candy mountain.

Chorus

4. In the big rock candy mountain,
All the jails are made of tin,
And you can break right out again
As soon as they throw you in.

There ain't no rakes nor shovels,
No axes, saws, nor picks.
I long to stay where they sleep all day,

Where they hanged the jerk
who invented work,
In the big rock candy mountain.

MICHAEL, ROW THE BOAT ASHORE

Chorus:
    Michael, row the boat
       ashore.
    Allelu-ia!
    Michael, row the boat
       ashore.
    Allelu-u-u-u-ia!

1. The River Jordan is
    chilly and cold.
  Allelu-ia!
  Chills the body, but
    not the soul.
  Allelu-u-u-u-ia!

    Chorus

2. River is deep, and
    the river is wide.

Allelu-ia!
Milk and honey on
   the other side.
Allelu-u-u-u-ia!

    Chorus

3. Brother, help me trim the sail.
  Allelu-ia!
  If we've faith, we cannot fail.
  Allelu-u-u-u-ia!

    Chorus

4. River is quick, and
    the river is fast.
  Allelu-ia!
  But we shall reach
    that shore at last.
  Allelu-u-u-u-ia!

    Chorus

5. Skies are black, and
    the wind's northwest.
  Allelu-ia!
  Grip that tiller and
    do your best.
  Allelu-u-u-u-ia!

    Chorus

6. Sister, help him lock the oar.
  Allelu-ia!
  And he'll row the boat
    ashore.
  Allelu-u-u-u-ia!

    Chorus

JIMMY CRACK CORN (The Blue-Tail Fly)

1. When I was young I used to wait
   On Master and hand him the plate
   And pass the bottle when he got dry
   And brush away the blue-tail fly.

Chorus:

   Jimmy crack corn, an' I don't care,
   Jimmy crack corn, an' I don't care,
   Jimmy crack corn, an' I don't care,
   Old Master's gone away.

2. Then after dinner he'd fall asleep
   And bid this servant vigil keep.
   And when he went to shut his eye,
   He'd tell me, "Watch the blue-tail fly."

   Chorus

3. And when he rode in the afternoon
   I followed with a hick'ry broom,
   The ponies being very shy
   When bitten by the blue-tail fly.

   Chorus

4. One day he rode around the farm,
   The flies so numerous they did swarm.
   One chanced to bite him on the thigh—
   The devil take that blue-tail fly!

   Chorus

5. The ponies run, they jump and pitch
   And tumble Master in the ditch.
   He died, and the jury wondered why.
   The verdict was: the blue-tail fly.

   Chorus

6. They laid him 'neath a 'simmon tree,
   His epitaph is there to see:
   "Beneath this stone I'm forced to lie,
   A victim of the blue-tail fly."

   Chorus

7. Old Master's gone—now let him rest.
   They say all things are for the best.
   I'll ne'er forget 'till the day I die
   Old Master and that blue-tail fly.

   Chorus

SHE'LL BE COMIN' 'ROUND THE MOUNTAIN

1. She'll be comin' 'round the mountain
When she comes.
She'll be comin' 'round the mountain
When she comes.
She'll be comin' 'round the mountain.
She'll be comin' 'round the mountain.
She'll be comin' 'round the mountain
When she comes.

2. She'll be driving six white horses
When she comes.
   [Repeat, as in first verse.]

3. She'll be shining bright as silver
When she comes.
   [Repeat, as in first verse.]

4. She will neither rock nor totter
When she comes.
   [Repeat, as in first verse.]

5. Oh, we'll all go out to meet her
When she comes.
   [Repeat, as in first verse.]

6. We will kill the old red rooster
When she comes.
   [Repeat, as in first verse.]

7. And we'll all have chicken and dumplings
When she comes.
   [Repeat, as in first verse.]

8. There'll be joy and smiles and laughter
When she comes.
   [Repeat, as in first verse.]

9. She will drive us all to Heaven
When she comes.
   [Repeat, as in first verse.]

10. But it may be just a while yet
'Fore she comes.
Yes, it may be just a while yet
'Fore she comes.
Oh, it may be just a while yet,
Yes, it may be just a while yet,
And it may be just a while yet
'Fore she comes.

 # BILLY BOY

1. "Oh, where have you gone,
   Billy Boy, Billy Boy?
   Oh, where have you gone,
   charming Billy?"
   "I have gone to seek a wife.
   She's the joy of my young life.

Chorus:
   She's a young thing,
   and cannot leave her mother."

2. "Did she ask you to come in,
   Billy Boy, Billy Boy?
   Did she ask you to come in,
   charming Billy?"
   "Yes, she asked me to come in.
   There's a dimple on her chin.

Chorus

3. "Did she pull for you a chair,
   Billy Boy, Billy Boy?
   Did she pull for you a chair,
   charming Billy?"
   "Yes, she pulled for me a chair,
   But its bottom was not there.

Chorus

4. "How tall does she stand,
   Billy Boy, Billy Boy?
   How tall does she stand,
   charming Billy?"
   "She is tall as a pumpkin vine,
   And as straight as oak or pine.

Chorus

5. "Are her eyes blue and bright,
   Billy Boy, Billy Boy?
   Are her eyes blue and bright,
   charming Billy?"
   "Yes, her eyes are blue and bright,
   But they're also minus sight.

Chorus

6. "Oh, how old is this lass,
   Billy Boy, Billy Boy?
   Oh, how old is this lass,
   charming Billy?"
   "She is threescore six or seven,
   Twenty-eight, nine, and eleven.

Chorus

7. "Does she often go to church,
   Billy Boy, Billy Boy?
   Does she often go to church,
   charming Billy?"
   "Yes, she often goes to church,
   In a bonnet white as birch.

Chorus

8. "Can she bake a cherry pie,
   Billy Boy, Billy Boy?
   Can she bake a cherry pie,
   charming Billy?"
   "Yes, she bakes a cherry pie
   Fast as you can wink your eye.

Chorus

9. "Can she fry a side of meat,
   Billy Boy, Billy Boy?
   Can she fry a side of meat,
   charming Billy?"
   "She can fry a side of meat
   Just as fast as you can eat.

Chorus

10. "Can she milk a Jersey calf,
    Billy Boy, Billy Boy?
    Can she milk a Jersey calf,
    charming Billy?"
    "She can milk a Jersey calf,
    And not miss the pail by half.

Chorus

11. "Can she milk a brindle cow,
    Billy Boy, Billy Boy?
    Can she milk a brindle cow,
    charming Billy?"
    "She can milk a brindle cow
    If her mother shows her how.

Chorus

12. "Can she bake a loaf of bread,
    Billy Boy, Billy Boy?
    Can she bake a loaf of bread,
    charming Billy?"
    "She can bake a loaf of bread
    That is bigger than your head.

Chorus

13. "Can she mend your denim britches,
    Billy Boy, Billy Boy?
Can she mend your denim britches,
    charming Billy?"
"She can mend my denim britches
Fast as I can count the stitches.

Chorus

14. "Can she stuff a bed with feathers,
    Billy Boy, Billy Boy?
Can she stuff a bed with feathers,
    charming Billy?"
"She can stuff a bed with feathers,
Only not in breezy weather.

Chorus

15. "Does she wear her hat with pins,
    Billy Boy, Billy Boy?
Does she wear her hat with pins,
    charming Billy?"
"Yes, I saw her go and pin it,
Though a hen was nesting in it.

Chorus

16. "Does she wear a string of pearls,
    Billy Boy, Billy Boy?
Does she wear a string of pearls,
    charming Billy?"
"Yes, she wears 'em as a favor—
They're the pearls her grandson gave her.

Chorus

17. "Are her teeth all clean and white,
    Billy Boy, Billy Boy?
Are her teeth all clean and white,
    charming Billy?"
"Yes, her teeth are clean and white,
'Cause she soaks them every night.

Chorus

18. "Is her leg quite slim and fine,
    Billy Boy, Billy Boy?
Is her leg quite slim and fine,
    charming Billy?"
"Yes, her leg is slim and fine—
Either oak, or ash, or pine.

Chorus

19. "Has she grown to be a beauty,
      Billy Boy, Billy Boy?
      Has she grown to be a beauty,
      charming Billy?"

"Well, maybe when she's older,
In the eye of the beholder.

Chorus

SWANEE RIVER (Old Folks at Home)

1. Way down upon the Swanee River
   Far, far away,
   That's where my heart is turning ever,
   There's where the old folks stay.
   All up and down the whole creation
   Sadly I roam
   Still longing for the old plantation
   And for the old folks at home.

Chorus:
   All the world is sad and dreary
   Everywhere I roam.
   Oh, witness how my heart grows weary,
   Far from the old folks at home.

2. All round the little farm I wandered
   When I was young.
   Then, many happy days I squandered,

Many the songs I sung.
When I was playing with my brother,
Happy was I.
Oh, take me to my kind old mother,
There let me live and die.

Chorus

3. One little hut among the bushes,
   One that I love,
   Still sadly to my memory rushes
   No matter where I rove.
   When will I see the bees a-humming
   All 'round the comb?
   When will I hear the banjo strumming
   Down in my dear old home?

Chorus

BATTLE HYMN OF THE REPUBLIC

1. Mine eyes have seen the glory
   Of the coming of the Lord:
   He is trampling out the vintage
   Where the grapes of wrath are stored.
   He hath loosed the fateful lightning
   Of His terrible swift sword.
   His truth is marching on.

Chorus:
   Glory! Glory hallelujah!
   Glory! Glory hallelujah!
   Glory! Glory hallelujah!
   His truth is marching on.

2. I have seen Him in the watchfires
   Of a hundred circling camps.
   They have builded Him an altar
   In the evening dews and damps.
   I can read His righteous sentence
   By the dim and flaring lamps:
   His day is marching on.

   Chorus

3. I have read a fiery gospel
   Writ in burnished rows of steel:

"As ye deal with my condemnors,
So with ye my grace shall deal."
Let the hero born of woman
Crush the serpent with his heel,
Since God is marching on.

   Chorus

4. He has sounded forth the trumpet
   That shall never call retreat.
   He is sifting out the hearts of men
   Before His judgment seat.
   Oh be swift, my soul, to answer Him!
   Be jubilant, my feet!
   Our God is marching on.

   Chorus

5. In the beauty of the lilies
   Christ was born across the sea,
   With a glory in His bosom
   That transfigures you and me.
   As He died to make men holy
   Let us die to make men free,
   While God is marching on.

   Chorus

YANKEE DOODLE BOY

I'm a Yankee Doodle Dan-dy,
A Yankee Doodle, do or die—
A real live nephew of my Uncle Sam's,
Born on the Fourth of July.
I've a Yankee Doodle sweetheart,

She's my Yankee Doodle joy.
Yankee Doodle came to London,
Just to ride the ponies;
I am the Yankee Doodle Boy.

WHEN THE SAINTS GO MARCHIN' IN

1. Oh, when the saints
   Go marchin' in,
   Oh, when the saints
   Go marchin' in,
   Oh, Lord, I want to be
     in that number,
   When the saints go
     marchin' in.

2. Oh, when the sun
   No longer shines,
   Oh, when the sun no
     longer shines,

Oh, Lord, I want to be
  in that number,
When the sun no
  longer shines.

3. Oh, when the moon
   Turns into blood. . . .

4. And when the new
   World is revealed. . . .

5. When Angel Gab-
   riel blows his horn. . . .

6. And when the rev-
   elation comes. . . .

7. And on that Hal-
   lelujah day. . . .

8. Oh, when they gather
   'Round the throne. . . .

9. And when the earth
   Has turned to flame. . . .

10. And when the dead
    Are raised again. . . .

    [Repeat first verse.]

POLLY WOLLY DOODLE

1. Oh, I went down South for to see my Sal.
   Sing "Polly-Wolly-Doodle" all the day.
   My Sal, she is a spunky gal.
   Sing "Polly-Wolly-Doodle" all the day.

Chorus:
   Fare thee well!
   Fare thee well!
   Fare thee well, my fairy fey.
   For I'm off to Louisiana
   For to see my Su-sy Anna,
   Singing "Polly-Wolly-Doodle" all the day.

2. Oh, my Sal she is a maiden fair.
   Sing "Polly-Wolly-Doodle" all the day.
   With curly eyes and laughing hair.
   Sing "Polly-Wolly-Doodle" all the day.

   Chorus

3. Oh, I came to a river and I couldn't get across.
   Sing "Polly-Wolly-Doodle" all the day.
   And I jumped upon a catfish and
      thought it was a horse.
   Sing "Polly-Wolly-Doodle" all the day.

Chorus

4. Oh, a grasshopper sitting on a railroad track.
   Sings "Polly-Wolly-Doodle" all the day,
   A-picking his teeth with a carpet tack.
   Sing "Polly-Wolly-Doodle" all the day.

   Chorus

5. Oh, I went to bed but it wasn't any use.
   Sing "Polly-Wolly-Doodle" all the day.
   My feet stuck out for a chicken roost.
   Sing "Polly-Wolly-Doodle" all the day.

   Chorus

6. Behind the barn down on my knees—
   Sing "Polly-Wolly-Doodle" all the day—
   I thought I heard a chicken sneeze.
   Sing "Polly-Wolly-Doodle" all the day.

   Chorus

7. He sneezed so hard with whooping cough—
   Sing "Polly-Wolly-Doodle" all the day—
   He sneezed his head and tail right off.
   Sing "Polly-Wolly-Doodle" all the day.

   Chorus

THE WABASH CANNON BALL

1. From the great Atlantic Ocean
   To the wide Pacific shore,
   From the green of blooming mountains
   To the ivy by the door.
   She's a-mighty tall and handsome
   And quite well-known by all.
   She's the modern combination—

Chorus:
   —On the Wabash Cannon Ball!

2. She came down from Birmingham
   One cold December day
   As she rolled into the station,
   You could hear the people say,
   "There's a girl from Tennessee.
   She's long and she is tall.
   She came down from Memphis—

   Chorus

3. Now the eastern states are dandy,
   So the western people say.
   From New York to St. Louis,

And Chicago on the way,
From the hills of Minnesota
Where the rippling waters fall,
No chances can be taken—

   Chorus

4. Will you listen to the whistle
   And the rumble and the roar,
   As she glides along the woodland,
   Through the hills and by the shore.
   Hear the throb of her great engine,
   Hear the lonesome hobos squall,
   "You're traveling through the jungle—

   Chorus

5. Here's to Daddy Klaxton!
   May his name forever stand,
   And always be remembered
   Round the courts of our great land.
   When his earthly race is over
   And the curtains round him fall,
   We shall carry him to glory—

   Chorus

TOM DOOLEY

Chorus:
    Hang down your head,
      Tom Dooley.
    Hang down your head
      and cry.
    Hang down your head,
      Tom Dooley.
    Poor Boy, you're bound
      to die.

1. I met her on the mountain
   In the month of May
   But for my jealous temper
   She'd be mine today.
       Chorus

2. I met her on the mountain
   There I took her life.
   Under a cliff of ivy,
   Stabbed her with my knife.
       Chorus

3. I dug a hole five feet long,
   Dug it five feet deep,
   Threw the earth on Annie,
   Tamped it with my feet.
       Chorus

4. See this watch of silver?
   Take it, if you will.
   See my mother gets it.
   Say I love her still.
       Chorus

5. Take down my old fiddle.
   Play it all you will.
   At this time tomorrow,
   I'll lie cold and still.
       Chorus

6. This time tomorrow
   Reckon where I'll be
   In some lonesome valley
   Swinging from a white
       oak tree.
       Chorus

7. Lay me in the graveyard
   Next to Annie Bell.
   We shall meet in Heaven,
   Or else we'll meet in Hell.
       Chorus

KOOKABURRA

1. Kookaburra sits in the old gum tree-ee.
   Merry, merry king of the bush is he-ee.
   Laugh, Kookaburra, laugh, Kookaburra,
   Gay your life must be.

2. Kookaburra, sits in an old gum tree-ee,
   Eating all the gumdrops he can see-ee.
   Stop, Kookaburra, stop, Kookaburra,
   Leave a few for me.

 # FROG, HE WENT A-COURTING

1. Frog, he went a-courting, and he did ride,
Unh-hunh, unh-hunh.
Frog, he went a-courting, and he did ride,
Unh-hunh, unh-hunh,
With sword and pistol by his side.
Unh-hunh, unh-hunh, unh-hunh.

2. He bridled and saddled a big striped snail,
Unh-hunh, unh-hunh.
He bridled and saddled a big striped snail,
Unh-hunh, unh-hunh,
And rode it 'tween the horns and tail.
Unh-hunh, unh-hunh, unh-hunh.

3. Rode the snail up to Miss Mouse's door,
Unh-hunh, unh-hunh.
[Repeat first two lines.]
Where he had often been before.
Unh-hunh, unh-hunh, unh-hunh.

4. He called, "Miss Mouse, are you within?"
Unh-hunh, unh-hunh.
[Repeat first two lines.]
"Yes, sir, for I'm sitting down to spin."
Unh-hunh, unh-hunh, unh-hunh.

5. Frog, he took Miss Mouse upon his knee,
Unh-hunh, unh-hunh.
[Repeat first two lines.]
And asked, "My dear, will you marry me?"
Unh-hunh, unh-hunh, unh-hunh.

6. "Why, without my Uncle Rat's consent,
Unh-hunh, unh-hunh.
[Repeat first two lines.]
I'd not marry e'en the president."
Unh-hunh, unh-hunh, unh-hunh.

7. Frog jumped on his snail and rode away,
Unh-hunh, unh-hunh.
[Repeat first two lines.]
Vowed to come back another day.
Unh-hunh, unh-hunh, unh-hunh.

8. Now Uncle Rat, when he came home,
Unh-hunh, unh-hunh.
[Repeat first two lines.]
Asked, "Who's been here since I was gone?"
Unh-hunh, unh-hunh, unh-hunh.

9. "A very fine frog's been calling here,
Unh-hunh, unh-hunh.
[Repeat first two lines.]
And asked me for to be his dear."
Unh-hunh, unh-hunh, unh-hunh.

10. Uncle Rat, he laughed and shook his sides,
Unh-hunh, unh-hunh.
[Repeat first two lines.]
To think his niece would be a bride.
Unh-hunh, unh-hunh, unh-hunh.

11. So Uncle Rat, he rode to town,
Unh-hunh, unh-hunh.
[Repeat first two lines.]
To buy Miss Mouse a wedding gown.
Unh-hunh, unh-hunh, unh-hunh.

12. Say where the wedding supper shall be,
Unh-hunh, unh-hunh.
[Repeat first two lines.]
Down by the river in a hollow tree.
Unh-hunh, unh-hunh, unh-hunh.

13. Say what the wedding supper shall be,
Unh-hunh, unh-hunh.
[Repeat first two lines.]

One green bean and a black-eyed pea.
Unh-hunh, unh-hunh, unh-hunh.

14. Tell us, how was Miss Mousie dressed,
Unh-hunh, unh-hunh.
[Repeat first two lines.]
In a cobweb veil and her Sunday best.
Unh-hunh, unh-hunh, unh-hunh.

15. Tell us next, what the Frog did wear,
Unh-hunh, unh-hunh.
[Repeat first two lines.]
Sky-blue pants and a doublet fair.
Unh-hunh, unh-hunh, unh-hunh.

16. The first guest to call was the bumblebee,
Unh-hunh, unh-hunh.
[Repeat first two lines.]
And played them a fiddle upon his knee.
Unh-hunh, unh-hunh, unh-hunh.

17. The next to come were the duck and drake,
Unh-hunh, unh-hunh.
[Repeat first two lines.]
Who ate every crumb of the wedding cake.
Unh-hunh, unh-hunh, unh-hunh.

18. "Come now, Mrs. Mouse, may we have
       some beer,
    Unh-hunh, unh-hunh.
    [Repeat first two lines.]
    That your uncle and I may have
       some cheer?"
    Unh-hunh, unh-hunh, unh-hunh.

19. "Pray, Mr. Frog, will you give us a song,
    Unh-hunh, unh-hunh.
    [Repeat first two lines.]
    That's bright and cheery and shan't
       last long?"
    Unh-hunh, unh-hunh, unh-hunh.

20. "Indeed, Mrs. Mouse," replied the Frog,
    Unh-hunh, unh-hunh.
    [Repeat first two lines.]
    "A cold has made me hoarse as a hog."
    Unh-hunh, unh-hunh, unh-hunh.

21. "Since a cold in the head has you laid up,
    Unh-hunh, unh-hunh.
    [Repeat first two lines.]
    I'll sing you a song that I just made up."
    Unh-hunh, unh-hunh, unh-hunh.

22. They all sat down and started to chat,
    Unh-hunh, unh-hunh.
    [Repeat first two lines.]
    When in came the kittens and the cat.
    Unh-hunh, unh-hunh, unh-hunh.

23. The bride, in fright, she runs up the wall,
    Unh-hunh, unh-hunh.
    [Repeat first two lines.]
    Turns her ankle and down she falls.
    Unh-hunh, unh-hunh, unh-hunh.

24. They all went a-sailing across the lake,
    Unh-hunh, unh-hunh.
    [Repeat first two lines.]
    And all got swallowed by a big black snake,
    Unh-hunh, unh-hunh, unh-hunh.

25. And the ones who escaped were one,
       two, three,
    Unh-hunh, unh-hunh.
    [Repeat first two lines.]
    The Frog, the Rat, and Miss Mousie.
    Unh-hunh, unh-hunh, unh-hunh.

26. The Mouse and the Frog went off to France,
Unh-hunh, unh-hunh.
[Repeat first two lines.]
And that's the end of their romance.
Unh-hunh, unh-hunh, unh-hunh.

27. There's bread and jam upon the shelf,
Unh-hunh, unh-hunh.
[Repeat first two lines.]
If you want some, just help yourself.
Unh-hunh, unh-hunh, unh-hunh.

JEANIE WITH THE LIGHT BROWN HAIR

1. I dream of Jeanie
   with the light brown hair
Borne like a vapor
   on the golden air.
I see her tripping where
   the bright streams play,
Gay as the flowers
   along her way.

Chorus:

   Many are the fond notes
   Her merry voice would pour,
   Echoed by the birds
      in the grove o'er and o'er.
   Ah! I dream of Jeanie
      with the light brown hair,

Afloat like vapor on
   the soft summer air.

2. I long for Jeanie
   with the day-dawn smile,
Radiant with gladness,
   warm with winning guile.
I hear her melodies attuned
   to love,
Warm as the sunlight
   lighting heav'n above.

      Chorus

3. I sigh for Jeanie
   when the daylight fades,
Hour when the shadow
   haunts the dewy glades,

And when the stars
   adorn the midnight skies,
I view their light as
   her own dear eyes.

      Chorus

4. Sighing like the night wind,
   and sobbing like the rain,
Waiting for my lost one
   who comes not again,
How I long for Jeanie,
   with my heart bowed low,
Never more to find her where
   the bright waters flow.

      Chorus

CAMPTOWN RACES (Going to Run All Night)

1. The Camptown ladies sing this song:
   Doo-dah! Doo-dah!
   Camptown racetrack's five miles long.
   Oh! Doo-dah day!
   I came down there with my hat caved in.
   Doo-dah! Doo-dah!
   I went back home with a pocket full of tin.
   Oh! Doo-dah day!

Chorus:
   Going to run all night! Going to run all day!
   I'll bet my money on the bobtail nag—
   Somebody bet on the bay.

2. The long-tail filly and the big black horse—
   Doo-dah! Doo-dah!
   They fly the track and they both cut across.
   Oh! Doo-dah day!
   The blind horse wallowed in a big mud hole—
   Doo-dah! Doo-dah!
   Can't touch bottom with a ten-foot pole.
   Oh! Doo-dah day!

Chorus

3. Old muley cow came onto the track—
   Doo-dah! Doo-dah!
   The bobtail flung her over his back.
   Oh! Doo-dah day!
   Then flew along like a railroad car
   Doo-dah! Doo-dah!
   Running a race with a shooting star.
   Oh! Doo-dah day!

Chorus

4. See them flying on a ten-mile heat—
   Doo-dah! Doo-dah!
   'Round the racetrack, then repeat.
   Oh! Doo-dah day!
   I won my money on the bobtail nag.
   Doo-dah! Doo-dah!
   I keep my money in an old tow-bag.
   Oh! Doo-dah day!

Chorus

BLOW THE MAN DOWN

1. As I was a-walkin' down Paradise Street,
   Singing way, hay, blow the man down,
   A saucy young maiden I chanced for to meet.
   Give me some time to blow the man down.

2. I asked, "Where're you bound?"
       She said, "Nowhere today,"
   Singing way, hay, blow the man down,
   "Now that's fine," I replied,
       "for I'm headed that way."
   Give me some time to blow the man down.

3. We entered an ale-house looked down
       on the sea,
   Singing way, hay, blow the man down,
   There stood a policeman who stared right
       at me,
   Give me some time to blow the man down.

4. Said he, "You're a pirate
       that flies the black flag,
   Singing way, hay, blow the man down,

You've robbed some poor Dutchmen
    and left them in rags."
Give me some time to blow the man down.

5. "Oh, Officer, Officer, you do me wrong,
   Singing way, hay, blow the man down,
   I'm a freshwater sailor just in from
       Hong Kong."
   Give me some time to blow the man down.

6. But they jailed me six months
       in Old Lexington Town,
   Singing way, hay, blow the man down,
   For fighting and kicking and knocking
       him down.
   Give me some time to blow the man down.

7. Come all you brave sailors
       who follow the sea,
   Singing way, hay, blow the man down,
   And join in a-singing this chanty with me!
   Give me some time to blow the man down!

'ROUND HER NECK SHE WEARS A YELLER RIBBON

1. 'Round her neck she wears a yeller ribbon.
   She wears it in the springtime and in the
       month of May
   And if you ask her, "Why the decoration?"
   She'll say, it's for her lover—
   Who is fur, fur away!
   Fur away! Fur away!
   She wears it for her lover, who is fur,
       fur away.

2. 'Round the park she walks a little baby.
   She walks him in the winter
   And the summer, so they say.
   And if you ask her why on earth she
       walks him,
   She walks him for her lover—
   Who is fur, fur away!
   Fur away! Fur away!
   She walks him for her lover, who is fur,
       fur away.

3. That boy, he is a cunning little feller.
   His birthday was a year ago,
   Late in the month of May.
   And if you ask him, "Sonny,
       who's your daddy?"

He'll say, "My dad's a cowboy—
Who is fur, fur away!
Fur away! Fur away!"
He'll say, "My dad's a cowboy who is fur,
    fur away."

4. Behind the door, her father keeps a shotgun.
   It's loaded with a double dose
   Of buckshot, so they say.
   And if you ask him, "Why the ammunition?"
   He keeps it for that cowboy—
   Who is fur, fur away!
   Fur away! Fur away!
   He keeps it for that cowboy, who is fur,
       fur away.

5. Now on a grave she lays a wreath of flowers.
   She lays it there in wintertime
   And in the month of May.
   And if you ask her who the wreath's
       to honor,
   She'll say, "It's for my lover—
   Who has gone fur away.
   Fur away! Fur away!"
   She'll say, "It's for my cowboy who has gone
       fur away."

JOHN BROWN'S BODY

1. John Brown's body lies
   a-mouldering in the grave,
   John Brown's body lies
   a-mouldering in the grave,
   John Brown's body lies
   a-mouldering in the grave,
   His soul goes marching on!

Chorus:

   Glory, glory hallelujah!
   Glory, glory hallelujah!
   Glory, glory hallelujah!
   His soul goes marching on!

2. Stars in Heaven are all
   looking kindly down,
   Stars in Heaven are all
   looking kindly down,
   Stars in Heaven are all
   looking kindly down,
   His soul goes marching on!

   Chorus

3. John Brown's knapsack is
   strapped upon his back,
   John Brown's knapsack is
   strapped upon his back,
   John Brown's knapsack is
   strapped upon his back,
   His soul goes marching on!

   Chorus

4. He's gone to be a soldier
   in the army of the Lord,
   He's gone to be a soldier
   in the army of the Lord,
   He's gone to be a soldier
   in the army of the Lord,
   His soul goes marching on!

   Chorus

OH, SUSANNA!

1. I came from Alabama with
   My banjo on my knee.
   I'm gone to Lou'siana
   My true love for to see.
   It rained all night
   the day I left.

   The weather, it was dry.
   The sun so hot
   I froze to death.
   Susanna, don't you cry!

Chorus:

   Oh, Susanna! Oh, don't
   you cry for me.
   I've come from Alabama
   with my banjo on my knee.

2. I jumped aboard the telegraph
   And traveled down the wires.
   The 'lectric fluid magnified

And lit five hundred fires.
The full moon burst,
  my horse ran off.
I really thought I'd die.
I shut my eyes to hold
  my breath.
Susanna, don't you cry!
      Chorus
3. I had a dream the other night
When everything was still

I thought I saw Susanna
A-coming down the hill.
A buckwheat cake was
  in her mouth
A tear was in her eye.
I said, "I'm coming
  from the South,
Susanna, don't you cry!"
      Chorus
4. I soon will be in New Orleans,

And then I'll look around,
And when I find Susanna,
I'll fall upon the ground.
But if I do not find my love,
Then surely I shall die.
But when I'm dead
  and six feet down,
Susanna, don't you cry!

      Chorus

HE'S GOT THE WHOLE WORLD IN HIS HANDS

1. He's got the whole world in His hands.
   He's got the whole wide world in His hands.
   He's got the whole world in His hands.

Chorus:

   He's got the whole world in His hands.

2. He's got the wind and the rain in His hands.
   He's got the wind and the rain in His hands.
   He's got the wind and the rain in His hands.

      Chorus

3. He's got the little tiny baby in His hands.
   He's got the little tiny baby in His hands.
   He's got the little tiny baby in His hands.

      Chorus

4. He's got you and me, brother, in His hands.
   He's got you and me, brother, in His hands.
   He's got you and me, sister, in His hands.

      Chorus

5. He's got the Sun and the Moon in His hands,

He's got the Sun and the Moon in His hands.
He's got the Moon and the stars in His hands.
 Chorus

6. He's got love and salvation in His hands.
 He's got love and salvation in His hands.
 He's got love and salvation in His hands.

Chorus

7. He's got everybody here in His hands.
 He's got everybody here in His hands.
 He's got everybody here in His hands.

 Chorus

THE CAISSON SONG (The Caissons Go Rolling Along)

1. Over hill, over dale
 We have hit the dusty trail,
 And those caissons go rolling along!
 In and out, hear them shout;
 Countermarch and round about,
 While those caissons go rolling along.

Chorus:

 Oh, it's hi, hi, hee
 For the field artillery.
 Shout out your numbers loud and strong.
  Two! Three! Four!
 And wherever you may go,
 You will always know

That the caissons go rolling along—
Keep 'em rolling!—
That the caissons are rolling along.

2. At the front, day and night,
 Where the doughboys dig and fight—
 And those caissons go rolling along!—
 Our barrage will be there,
 Adding to the rockets' glare,
 While the caissons go rolling along.

 Chorus

3. Hear that whine? It's a shell!
 Hit the dirt and dig like hell,
 While the caissons go rolling along.

Comes the boom, stand up higher,
Take good aim, return the fire,
Help those caissons go rolling along!

    Chorus

4. Through the mud, through the lines,

Past the trenches and the mines,
Where the caissons go rolling along.
We won't rest till we see
Our brave lads taste victory,
And the caissons stop rolling along.
    Chorus

MEET ME IN ST. LOUIS, LOUIS

1. When Louis came to the flat,
He hung up his coat and his hat.
He gazed all around, but no wifey he found,
So he asked, "Where can Flossie be at?"
A note on the table he spied.
He read it just once, then he cried.
It ran, "Louis dear,
It's too slow for me here,
So I think I will go for a ride.

Chorus:

"Meet me in St. Louis, Louis,
Meet me at the Fair.
Don't tell me that lights are shining
Any place but there.

We will dance the Hootchee Kootchie,
I will be your tootsie wootsie,
If you will meet me in St. Louis, Louis,
Meet me at the Fair."

2. The dresses that hung in the hall
Were gone—she had taken them all.
She took all his rings, and
    the rest of his things.
The picture he missed from the wall.
"What, moving?" the janitor said.
"Your rent is paid three months ahead!"
"What good is the flat?"
Asked poor Louis, "Read that!"
And the janitor smiled as he read:
    Chorus

HOME, SWEET HOME

1. 'Midst pleasures and palaces
   Though we may roam,
   Be it ever so humble,
   There's no place like home!
   A charm from the skies
   Seems to hallow us there
   Which, seek through
     the world,
   Is ne'er met with elsewhere.

Chorus:
   Home! Home! Sweet,
     sweet home!
   There's no place like home!
   There's no place like home!

2. I gaze on the moon
   As I tread the drear wild,
   And feel that my mother
   Now thinks of her child;
   As she looks on that moon
   From our own cottage door
   Through the woodbine
     whose fragrance
   Will cheer me no more.

   Chorus

3. An exile from home
   Splendor dazzles in vain.
   Oh, give me my lowly
   Thatched cottage again!
   The birds singing gaily
   That came at my call—
   Give me them with the
     peace of mind
   Dearer than all.

   Chorus

4. How sweet 'tis to sit
   'Neath a fond father's smile,
   The caress of a mother
   To soothe and beguile.
   Let others delight
   'Midst new pleasures to roam,
   But give me, oh, give me
   The pleasures of home.

   Chorus

5. To thence I'll return,
   Overburdened with care.
   My heart's dearest solace
   Will smile on me there.
   No more from that cottage
   Again will I roam.
   Be it ever so humble,
   There's no place like home!

   Chorus